Ever After

How to Overcome Cynical

Students

with the Role of Wonder in

Education

Stephen R. Turley, Ph.D.

TURLEY TALKS

A New Conservative Age is Rising

www.turleytalks.com

Table of Contents

INTRODUCTION

Modern education is saturated with cynicism and skepticism. It's not uncommon to hear students complain with questions like: "When will I ever use calculus?" or "What do we have to learn this for anyway?" With modernist sensibilities dominated by utilitarianism and pragmatism, education is assumed to have value solely for its social usefulness and economic benefits. Unfortunately, with emphasis on grades, SAT scores, and the advantages provided by the 'tools of learning,' even classical educators, students, and parents are not immune from these utilitarian tendencies.

I believe that this modern cynicism can be effectively countered by introducing students to a fundamentally different world made up of a fundamentally different way of knowing. This world comprises what we might call a 'cosmology of wonder,' which offers a profoundly beautiful and inviting alternative to the frames of reference that generate and sustain cynicism.

In what follows, we will explore classical curriculum as a journey towards encountering the splendor of God. For classical educators and philosophers, a correct knowledge of this world was rooted in a kind of intellectual *eros*, a cognitive love or desire to encounter the world as a reflection of divine life. Common to both the classical tradition and the Church, the human person experienced *eros* or love through the evocation of wonder, what the Greeks called *thauma*, itself evoked by encountering the eternal values of Truth, Goodness, and Beauty.

We will learn how to overcome cynicism by teaching students to view the world as a divine arena of wonder and awe. In Part I, we will examine cynicism, fairy tales, and the world of wonder. Chapter one identifies two reasons why contemporary students are so cynical. Chapter two explores the essay, "The Ethics of Elfland," by G.K. Chesterton, and how fairy tales awaken us to a world of wonder. In chapter three, we will discover the relatively recent recovery of classical education, and how such a recovery enables students to see divine meaning and purpose in every facet of life. In Part II, I will provide practical suggestions for how to effectively teach this world of wonder to our students. Chapter four introduces us to the relationship between Beauty and love. Chapter five provides an overview of teaching students to see the world anew through your subject. Chapter six lists suggestions for cultivating a beautiful culture in your schools and classrooms.

My hope is that by encountering the world as a divine gift, our students will begin to see all things in light of the one in whom all things are made new, and know that it is their calling indeed to be astonished and astounded.

Part I

Cynical Students, Fairy Tales, and the World of Wonder

CHAPTER 1

Two Reasons Students are Cynical

"And every time you look up in the sky," I was telling my Biblical Theology class, "and see birds flying above with their wings stretched out in the form of a cross, and flying in a V-formation, you will be reminded of the victory of Christ's cross over sin, death, and the devil."

"How do you know that?" one of my students responds. "How do we know that there is any correspondence between the letter 'v,' birds, and the cross?"

As teachers or homeschooling parents, I doubt you have encountered this particular classroom scenario, but we all have to deal at some point with the cynical student. Indeed, cynicism may be considered by many teachers the default posture of a number if not most of our students. Simply put, there is nothing more soul-draining for a teacher than an encounter with flippant irreverent students.

What's behind this cynicism? Why are students so often unimpressed and dismissive towards subjects that we love?

There are two main reasons our students are cynical:

1. They know only through doubting. The rise of the Enlightenment in the eighteenth-century brought with it a new way of knowing the world: knowledge was limited solely to that which could be verified by a *method*, namely, the application of science and reason. It was argued that only those things that could be verified by the empirical method were those things that could be known in a way that was completely detached from the preconceptions of the observer. Anything that was not subjected to or failed this method was reduced to the state of person-relativity and excluded from the arena of what can be known. Thus knowledge was now open to man: all he had to do, in any area of life, was to apply the method.

Now, there is an important pattern here. From this methodological vantage point, knowledge is rooted in doubt. In other words, I have the right to doubt anything unless it can be proven to me otherwise. True knowledge comes about only when doubt has been left behind.

2. They see all meaning systems as fabricated. With the rise of a new definition of knowledge confined to the scientific method, all sense of meaning and purpose in the world disappears. Because divine meaning and purpose are impervious to the scientific method they cannot be known, and so it became increasingly plausible to see the world as comprised of cause and effect processes that have no meaning apart from that which people personally or culturally chose to project upon it.

What this means is that students intuit that all cultural rules, all social laws, are inherently arbitrary; they don't reflect any transcendent cosmic moral order and are there only because some people have the power to put them there. And thus human relationships are irreducibly comprised of arbitrary power relationships

Now, I believe that these two frames of reference, doubt influenced knowledge and dreamed up meaning, coalesce to birth a profound sense that nothing is what it is cracked up to be, and that all human relationships involve some degree of manipulation and coercion.

And it is these two frames of reference that largely inform how our students interpret academic expectations on the one hand and the various rules, practices and etiquettes that constitute our school life on the other.

On the one hand, because knowledge is rooted in doubt, the teacher or the administrator is naturally put on the defensive; you the teacher have to prove to me the student that this book or music or class is something worth my time and attention. Otherwise stop wasting my time.

And on the other hand, the formal standards and rules of the school are naturally perceived as arbitrary, since there is no objective meaning and purpose in the world that holds all things together. Our students have a tacit understanding that all rules and academic expectations are arbitrary and are there only because some people have the power to put them there.

So, how do we as educators and parents respond to this cynicism rooted in doubt and power?

I believe that this modern cynicism can be effectively countered by introducing students to a fundamentally different world made up of a fundamentally different way of knowing. This world comprises what we might call a 'cosmology of wonder', which offers a profoundly beautiful and inviting alternative to the frames of reference fundamental to the generating and sustaining of cynicism.

Wonder is awakened by inviting our students to receive the world as a gift. For example, if students see the world as mere arbitrary physical processes with no inherent meaning, then students can rightly expect that the teacher has to convince them that this class, or book, or subject material is worth their time and attention.

But if the world is a gift, if the world is filled with divine meaning and purpose, and if this class, or book, or subject material awakens us to that divine meaning and purpose, then both teacher and students approach this class, or book, or subject material not as something worth our time, *but rather as something of which we are not worthy.*

So how do we teach a cosmology of wonder?

To answer that question, we shall turn to G.K. Chesterton and his masterful essay, "The Ethics of Elfland," where we will learn about the role of wonder in rightly understanding our world.

CHAPTER 2

The World through Stories and Spectacles

In his masterful essay, "The Ethics of Elfland," G. K. Chesterton treats us to an extended meditation on a body of literature that was to be one of the most significant factors in his Christian conversion: the fairy tale. Because fairy tales awaken within us a remembrance of the wonder and awe that once filled our hearts when we first encountered the world around us, Chesterton concluded that fairy tales were revelatory of the fact that it is part of our nature as humans to be astonished and astounded. Chesterton writes:

> ... we all like astonishing tales because they touch the nerve of the ancient instinct of astonishment. This is proved by the fact that when we are very young children we do not need fairy tales: we only need tales. Mere life is interesting enough. A child of seven is excited by being told that Tommy opened a door and saw a dragon. But a child of three is excited by being told that Tommy opened a door. Boys like romantic

tales; but babies like realistic tales--because they find them romantic. In fact, a baby is about the only person, I should think, to whom a modern realistic novel could be read without boring him. This proves that even nursery tales only echo an almost pre-natal leap of interest and amazement. These tales say that apples were golden only to refresh the forgotten moment when we found that they were green. They make rivers run with wine only to make us remember, for one wild moment, that they run with water... We have all forgotten what we really are.... All that we call spirit and art and ecstasy only means that for one awful instant we remember that we forget.[1]

Chesterton's essay, however, is not interested in merely recounting the role of wonder in his coming to Christian faith; rather, Chesterton very deliberately contrasts this defining role of wonder with its distinctive absence from the modern age. Chesterton, in his characteristic wit and insight, actually goes so far as to identify the loss of wonder, the absence of astonishment, as the key characteristic of the modern age. He demonstrates this wonderlessness by contrasting the world as seen through the eyes of a child, what he calls 'Elfland', and the world as seen through the spectacles of the modernist, what he calls the 'Natural World'. Chesterton writes:

> There are certain sequences or developments ... which are, in the true sense of the word, reasonable. They are, in the true sense of the word, necessary. Such are mathematical and merely logical sequences. We in fairyland (who are the most reasonable of all creatures)

---

[1] G.K. Chesterton, *Orthodoxy* (Garden City, NY: Image Book, 1959), 54.

admit that reason and that necessity. For instance, if the Ugly Sisters are older than Cinderella, it is ... necessary that Cinderella is younger than the Ugly Sisters. There is no getting out of it. .. If Jack is the son of a miller, a miller is the father of Jack.... If the three brothers all ride horses, there are six animals and eighteen legs involved: that is true rationalism, and fairyland is full of it. But as I put my head over the hedge of the elves and began to take notice of the natural world, I observed an extraordinary thing. I observed that learned men in spectacles were talking of the actual things that happened-- dawn and death and so on--as if they were rational and inevitable. They talked as if the fact that trees bear fruit were just as necessary as the fact that two and one trees make three. But it is not. There is an enormous difference by the test of fairyland; which is the test of the imagination. You cannot imagine two and one not making three. But you can easily imagine trees not growing fruit; you can imagine them growing golden candlesticks or tigers hanging on by the tail. These men in spectacles spoke much of a man named Newton, who was hit by an apple, and who discovered a law. But they could not be got to see the distinction between a true law, a law of reason, and the mere fact of apples falling. If the apple hit Newton's nose, Newton's nose hit the apple. That is a true necessity: because we cannot conceive the one occurring without the other. But we can quite well conceive the apple not falling on his nose; we can fancy it flying ardently through the air to hit some other nose, of which it had a more definite dislike. We have always in our fairy tales kept this sharp distinction between the science of mental relations, in which there really are laws, and the science of physical facts, in which there are no laws, but only weird repetitions. We believe in bodily miracles, but not in mental impossibilities. We believe that a Bean-stalk climbed up to Heaven; but that does not at all confuse our convictions on the philosophical question of how many beans make five.[2]

For Chesterton, there is nothing more destructive to wonder and astonishment than the idolatrous worship of *facts*. For in the modernist pursuit of facts, one must dispel a rampant doubt and skepticism; one must, in good Cartesian fashion, doubt everything until one finds that which can no longer be doubted. But an epistemology built on doubt and skepticism places one in the incurably arrogant position as judge and jury over the world. Chesterton noticed that, in the ethics of Elfland, in the imagination of wonder and awe, there was not this attitude of cynical judgment. We see this in what Chesterton calls the Doctrine of Conditional Joy. According to elfin ethics all virtue resides in an 'if': 'You may live in a palace of gold and sapphire, *if* you do not say the word 'cow'; or 'You may go to the royal ball *if* you return by midnight'. Chesterton notes that nowhere in the ethics of Elfland is such a Doctrine of Conditional Joy ever challenged, questioned, or treated as unjust. If Cinderella were to have the audacity to interrogate, 'How is it that I must leave the ball at twelve?' her godmother might answer, 'How is it that you are going there till twelve?' You see, because the condition is never more eccentric than the gift, no less fantastic, no more inexplicable than the wonder of existence itself, the child never asks, 'How come'? This is because the child has not

---

[2] Chesterton, *Orthodoxy*, 51.

been taught in the ways of the modernist, the wondrous eyes have yet to be blinded by the spectacles of the skeptic.

Modern Education: The World of Spectacles and the Turn toward the Self

This learned blindness is, unfortunately, on display every year in the education system of the West. Every school year begins with tens of thousands of Kindergarteners walking expectantly into school with their eyes filled with awe and wonder, and every school year ends with a graduating class made up of epistemological, moral, and aesthetic relativists who dismiss with characteristic flippancy, irreverence, and cynicism anything that purports to be pure, lovely, and virtuous, and we audaciously call this soul-draining process 'education'. Malcom Muggeridge was fond of saying that we have in fact educated ourselves into imbecility.[3] Both Muggeridge and Chesterton recognized that this educated imbecility was the result of an unprecedented and frankly radical experiment in human civilization. We in the west are in the midst of a collective social experiment that is attempting to construct a civilization based solely on scientifically observed cause and effect processes irrespective of any divinely-gifted transcendent meaning. Rooted in Enlightenment conceptions, it was argued that the enthronement of reason and method would finally realize what humans have hitherto for attempted to achieve through religious pursuits, but to no avail: wars would end, prosperity and technological advance would reign, and social and economic equality was finally within reach.

---

[3] Malcolm Muggeridge, *Seeing Through the Eye: Malcolm Muggeridge on Faith* (San Francisco: Ignatius Press, 2005), 16.

And so how does education fit into this social scientific experiment? In the satirical film, *The Gods Must Be Crazy*, the movie opens with a narrator who in Rousseauian fashion contrasts the primitive yet placid society of the tribal Bushmen with that of the confused urbanized modernist, and his description of modern life is very illuminating:

> Civilized man refused to adapt himself to his environment. Instead he adapted his environment to suit him. So he built cities, roads, vehicles, machinery. And he put up power lines to run his labor-saving devices. But somehow he didn't know when to stop. The more he improved his surroundings to make his life easier, the more complicated he made it. So now his children are sentenced to ten to fifteen years of school just to learn how to survive in this complex and hazardous habitat they were born into. And civilized man, who refused to adapt himself to his natural surroundings, now finds that he has to adapt and re-adapt himself, every hour of the day, to his self-created environment. For instance, if the day is called "Monday" and the number seven-three-zero comes up, you have to dis-adapt yourself from your domestic surroundings, and re-adapt yourself to an entirely different environment in the workplace. Eight-double-zero means everybody has to look busy. Ten-three-zero means you can stop looking busy for fifteen minutes. And then, you have to look busy again. And so your day is chopped up into little pieces. And in each segment of time you have to adapt to a new set of circumstances. No wonder some people go off the rails a bit.

This satirical commentary in fact foregrounds precisely how we moderns view education. Education in the modern age has been reduced to the learning of a set of social and technological life skills concomitant with a modern society, with the value of education measured proportionate to its social and economic usefulness. Now, I am not for a moment suggesting that computer labs, SATs, electives, and AV resources are bad, nor am I arguing that education should not have practical and technical relevance to the world in which we live. What I am concerned with is the dehumanizing effects of a pragmatism and utilitarianism gone mad. When computer labs and SAT scores and college transcripts and grade point averages mutate from mere servants to dominical masters, they in fact sever our educational pursuits from the transcendent, from that which is True, Good, and Beautiful regardless of time or culture. And the consequence of amputating education from the transcendent, which is evident throughout our modern society, is the inward introspectionist turn toward the self for meaning and life.

Today, it is ubiquitously believed that the self needs to be cultivated and nurtured, and in this process of turning toward the self, there has emerged a sense of entitlement to self-actualization, and an accompanying right to charge with malice anyone or anything that would seek to stifle the self. The result of this national collective self-indulgence is what researchers have called in a recent publication "The Narcissism Epidemic." The authors of this study have noted "a single underlying shift in the American psychology: Not only are there more narcissists than ever, but non-narcissistic people are seduced by the increasing emphasis on material wealth, physical appearance, celebrity worship, and attention seeking." How far self-infatuation has become a virtue in our culture was captured profoundly by Ralph Schoenstein in his article, "The Modern Mount Rushmore." Schoenstien writes:

> One-day last spring I stood before 20 children of eight and nine in [a] third-grade class to see if any heroes or heroines were inspiring them. I asked each child to give me the names of the three greatest people he had ever heard about. "Michael Jackson, Brooke Shields and Boy George," said a small blond girl, giving me one from all three sexes. "Michael Jackson, Spider-Man and God," a boy then said, naming a new holy trinity.... When the other children recited, Michael Jackson's name was spoken again and again, but Andrew Jackson never, nor Washington, Lincoln or any other presidential immortal. Just Ronald Reagan, who made it twice, once behind Batman and once behind Mr. T ...In answer to my request for heroes, I had expected to hear such names as Michael Jackson, Mr. T, Brooke Shields and Spider-Man from the kids, but I had not expected the replies of the eight who answered "Me." Their heroes were themselves. It is sad enough to see the faces on Mount Rushmore replaced by rock stars, brawlers and cartoons, but it is sadder still to see Mount Rushmore replaced by a mirror.[4]

This is why our students our so skeptical and cynical. If a world devoid of any inherent meaning and purpose, everything ends up revolving around the self. The self alone provides the human person with meaning. And if that is the case, then anything offered in an educational curriculum must

---

[4] Ralph Schoenstein, "The Modern Mount Rushmore," *Newsweek* 6 August, 1984.

past the test of the student's sovereign self. The parent or teacher is put in the position of having to convince students that this class, or book, or subject material is worth their time and attention. Nothing has any meaning or value in itself; such meaning or value can only be imparted by the student once his or her default doubt and skepticism has been dispelled.

But what if there were another way of looking at the world? What if this meaningless and purposeless world was a fiction, itself a rather sterile, indifferent, apathetic story hardly worth the student's time and attention? What if the world in which we live is actually a magical realm created to astonish and astound?

CHAPTER 3

The Role of Wonder in Classical Education

Chesterton's observations on the role of wonder in our humanity are not novel nor are they exceptional; they in fact echo the observations of the classical philosophers, for whom wonder was indeed indispensable in the pursuit of knowledge. For Plato, knowledge was rooted in what he considered a kind of intellectual *eros*, a cognitive desire to encounter the world as a reflection of divine life. Or as Socrates declared in Plato's *Theaetetus*: 'Philosophy begins in wonder and Iris [who is the messenger of heaven] is the child of wonder [*Thauman*]' (155d). According to Aristotle, wonder stimulates all thought and defines best why it is that we freely seek to know the world and its causes. In his *Metaphysics* Aristotle writes: 'it is owing to their wonder that men both now begin and at first began to philosophize' (982b). In the words of humanities professor, Richard Harp: "The classical tradition regarded wonder as both the origin and permanent companion of all rational inquiry. Wonder ... was ... considered a truly rational movement of the mind towards fresh knowledge."[5]

In contrast to our infatuation with self-esteem, it was classically understood that wonder began with an admission of personal impoverishment, what the Greeks called *aporia* and the Latins *pietas*. This in fact is the rationale for the Socratic Dialogue; Socrates is able to impart wisdom only when his interlocutor admits ignorance and perplexity. This intellectual and spiritual vacuousness, this virtue of humility, can then be *filled*, and filled not merely with facts that correspond to purposeless natural or social processes of cause and effect, but with a knowledge of the world as it relates to that which is eternally True, Good, and Beautiful. Plato in his *Timeaus* proposed that the contemplation of the cosmos could lead the soul to God and hence transcend the cosmos, a concept echoed in Aristotle's *De Philosophia*. This is because, for the classical tradition, the world and the cosmos were what we call in theology 'diaphanous', that is, all of creation is a temporal reflection of the eternal Beauty of the divine. And it was the role of culture to provide substantial, palpable, material manifestations of divine reality embedded in the cosmic order. Hence philosophy, history, logic, dialectic, rhetoric, aesthetics, physics, epic, lyric, comedy, democracy (all Greek words!) were means by which one could tangibly encounter *telos*, the divinely infused meaning and purpose embedded in the created order. And education, *paideia* in the Greek world, was precisely the initiation into this culture, for it is through embodying Greek culture that one was able to encounter divine life.

---

[5] Richard L. Harp, '*The Winter's Tale*: An "Old Tale" Begetting Wonder' Dalhousie Review 58 [1978], 295-308, 295.

As an extension of *paideia*, Graeco-Roman classical education understood each subject in what was termed the *trivium* (grammar, dialectic, rhetoric) and *quadrivium* (arithmetic, geometry, music, astronomy) as a subsidiary means, an instrumental portal, if you will, that enabled one to encounter realities that were not specific to any single time or place precisely because they were eternal and divine. The septet of liberal arts were inextricably bound to a diaphanous world, a creation that manifested temporally and spatially God's eternal Beauty, since the whole purpose of the *trivium* and *quadrivium* was to provide those lenses through which students could see this divine splendor in creation and hence cultivate a sense of their place in the cosmos. And because the world reflected an eternal dimension, the classical mind recognized, in the words of patristic scholar Andrew Louth, that true wisdom is beyond the grasp of the finite creature, man, and is indeed the possession of the gods. Knowledge in its traditional sense begins in wonder and in fact ends in wonder, since one is penetrating more deeply into the mystery of reality. Hence the term *philosophia*: the 'love of wisdom'. Impelled by this love for wisdom, Josef Pieper comments, "wonder is not just the starting point of philosophy in the sense of *initium*, of a prelude or preface. Wonder is the *principium*, the lasting source, the *fons et origo*, the immanent origin of philosophy ... The inner form of philosophizing is virtually identical with the inner form of wonder."[6]

The Cosmology Behind the Liberal Arts

---

[6] Quoted in Andrew Louth, *Discerning the Mystery: An Essay on the Nature of Theology* (Oxford: Clarendon Press, 1983), 144.

Now, the seven liberal arts, the *trivium* and *quadrivium*, are not arbitrary. They reveal the divine beauty inherent in the created order precisely because the *trivium* and *quadrivium* embody that created order. Whether we read the Genesis creation account, the Babylonain Enuma Elish, the Hermopolis cosmology of Egypt, or Hesiod's *Theogony*, the process of creation involves the shaping and ordering of unorganized matter by and in accordance with divine words, divine language. Because words order the material world, the Hellenist conception of the *Logos* was a rational order that held the cosmos together, a linguistic order that was in turn able to be discovered by men through use of the rationality they possess by virtue of their possession of language. The *Logos* was in fact a rational word, or linguistic order. Hence, if one is going to encounter this cosmos as a theater of divine beauty one must approach it, unpack as it were, with tools indicative of creation, with word and number, language and metric, *trivium* and *quadrivium*.

The cosmological significance of the rational word or linguistic order of the *Logos* provides then the foundation for cultural pursuits. Greek and Latin are transformed into languages that not only provide philosophical categories and scientific taxonomies, but they do so as such are inextricably linked to the language of prayer and adoration as it resounded throughout the Byzantine and Latin worlds for over a millennium and continues to this day in liturgies, poetry, and in the great choral works of the classical masters in relation to which there stands no equal. We often forget that Bach, in addition to teaching music, was also a teacher of Latin. As Tracy Lee Simmons has observed in his apologetic for Greek and Latin,[7] it was through the study of language, particularly in the declension and conjugation of words, that attentiveness, concentration, and contemplation were shaped within the student, and I would argue this is because the student is encountering in the verbal sign a microcosm of the very means by which the form and matter of the cosmos came to be ordered in the linguistic symmetry of the *Logos*.

Now, contrast this vision with modernist attitudes toward the study of languages. How many times have you heard the complaint, "Why would I want to study Latin, after all it's a dead language?" I find this so fascinating, because when I was in school, the argument was "Why do I have to study French? I have no plans of ever going to France!" In other words, the utilitarian approach despises the study of languages both living and dead! But what the utilitarian conception simply cannot comprehend – because it does not have the necessary frames of reference – is that concomitant with its creational significance, language awakens our humanity. Hence Adam's first act of dominion is *naming*, as an extension of God's naming his creation, calling the light 'day' and the darkness 'night'. Language enables us to escape the limitations of sheer animal instinct and the tyranny of the here and now, and makes real the discovery of other realms of which dumb creatures could never conceive, those of the possible, the plausible, the desirable, the valuable, the hopeful. As anthropologist Roy Rappaport observes, the worlds in which we humans live are not limited to solely tectonic,

---

[7] Tracy Lee Simmons, *Climbing Parnassus: A New Apologia for Greek and Latin* (Wilmington, DE: Intercollegiate Studies Institute, 2002).

meteorological and organic processes.[8] Our world is not only made of rocks and trees and oceans, but also of cosmologies, institutions, rules, and values. With language the world comes to be furnished with qualities like good and evil, abstractions like democracy and communism, values like honor and chivalry. Hence, language is a metaphysical reality with a transcendent origin. This is what Solzhenitsyn meant when he said: "One word of truth outweighs the world."[9]

This cosmic significance of language foregrounds how Grammar, Dialectic, and Rhetoric – that is, vocabulary, logic, and beauty – were inextricably linked with the metrical order and symmetry represented in the *quadrivium*: for the classical mind, arithmetic revealed 'number in itself', geometry revealed 'number in space', music revealed 'number in time', and astronomy revealed 'number in space and time'.[10] The *quadrivium* came alive as it were in classical Christian culture, particularly in its art and architecture. The dome on top of churches is the circular representation of the heavenly eternity, never beginning or ending, joined to the sanctuary or nave below by four great columns, signifying the four elements of the cosmos – earth, air, fire, and water – organized in terms of north, south, east, and west, echoing back to the four rivers that flowed out from Eden which transformed into baptismal waters through the four gospels going to the four corners of the world. This is why you see

---

[8] Roy A. Rappaport, *Ritual and Religion in the Making of Humanity* (Cambridge: Cambridge University Press, 1999), 8.

[9] http://www.nobelprize.org/nobel_prizes/literature/laureates/1970/solzhe nitsyn-lecture.html.

[10] See the excellent study on the classical *quadrivium* in Stratford Caldecott, *Beauty for Truth's Sake: On the Re-enchantment of Education* (Grand Rapids: Brazos Press, 2009).

particularly in Byzantine churches icons of the four evangelists on the four columns that unite heaven and earth, the dome with the sanctuary floor. The baptismal font itself was often shaped as an octagon, signifying the eighth-day, the day in which the Jews believed God would send his Messiah to restore the marred seven-day creation. As David Clayton points out, the very time we worship, Sunday, is simultaneously the first day of the new 7-day week and the eighth day that has liberated us from the previous week.[11] Our seven days of the week correspond to the seven heavens in medieval cosmology: the sun, the moon, Mercury, Venus, Mars, Jupiter, and Saturn which, in Dante's schema, corresponded to the seven liberal arts and thus, following Augustine, functioned as a weekly seven-step ascent to encountering wisdom (Lat. *sapienta*). And that cosmology entailed the mathematical ratios that provided the music of the spheres, which was reproduced on earth through analogous intervallic ratios, with the cosmic music resounding throughout the church thereby reconstituting the worshippers into participants of the worship of heaven. And of course, this worship took place in churches that were constructed classically facing East, the ascent of our words and song paralleling the rising of the sun, and hence both cathedral and creation praise God together in anticipation of the new creation.

It is amazing to me, and frankly somewhat discouraging, that at the Christian university where I teach, I have students -- who have spent their whole lives in the church -- walking into my classroom every semester who know everything about

---

[11] David Clayton, "The Path to Heaven is a Triple Helix," available at http://thewayofbeauty.org/2010/04/the-path-to-heaven-is-a-triple-helix/.

Earth Day and about 'going green', and yet they have no idea why churches classically face East, no idea of the significance of domes or the square or cruciform floor plans, no concept of the meaning of numbers or geometric theology, no concept of the vestment color scheme, or the liturgical calendar organizing theological themes around the seasons, and certainly and perhaps most characteristically no concept of a worship music that is as permanent and timeless as the heavenly spheres they resound. Thus, while so many of our students think they are more in touch with the environment than any other previous generation, the fact is that it is just the opposite! They as modernists are profoundly alienated from their ecology! They have been conditioned by their schools to think of the world around them as cause and effect processes devoid of any inherent meaning apart from the meaning they choose to give it; a world that exists either to be conquered by our machines on the one hand or protected as a fragile organism on the other. As such, our students are deprived of encountering creation, in Chesterton's words, as God's theatrical encore of childlike wonder:

> The thing I mean can be seen, for instance, in children, when they find some game or joke that they specially enjoy. ... Because children have abounding vitality, because they are in spirit fierce and free, therefore they want things repeated and unchanged. They always say, "Do it again"; and the grown-up person does it again until he is nearly dead. For grown-up people are not strong enough to exult in monotony. But perhaps God is strong enough to exult in monotony. It is possible that God says every morning, "Do it again" to the sun; and every evening, "Do it again" to the moon. It may not be automatic necessity that makes all daisies alike;

it may be that God makes every daisy separately, but has never got tired of making them. It may be that He has the eternal appetite of infancy; for we have sinned and grown old, and our Father is younger than we.[12]

The Universe of Narnia

For me, no one exemplifies this childlike wonder more than the classically educated C. S. Lewis. In a recent publication on Lewis entitled *Planet Narnia*, Michael Ward demonstrates from Lewis' other writings that Lewis was very much in love with the aesthetic and imaginative beauty of the medieval geocentric cosmos of the seven heavens.[13] In medieval cosmology, represented by astronomy in the *quadrivium* – and you had to study the heavens because where else would we get our music theory from – the seven observable planets embodied seven spiritual states. Jupiter embodies regal splendor and majesty; it is the planet of kings and prosperity. Mars influenced warriors by combining two otherwise incompatible virtues: bravery and gentleness which formed the medieval conception of chivalry. And while Jupiter is the king, it is the sun (yes, the sun is a planet in this cosmology) that is associated with the noblest metal, gold, and is the eye and mind of the whole universe. Luna, the moon, is the great frontier that divides the heavens from the earth, whose metal is silver, and because of its transience, its positional ambiguity between heaven and earth, the moon represents instability, hence the term 'lunatic'. Mercury is the Latin equivalent of Hermes, the messenger god, who was responsible for language, interpretation, and order. Venus,

---

[12] Chesterton, *Orthodoxy*, 60.
[13] Michael Ward, *Planet Narnia: The Seven Heavens in the Imagination of C.S. Lewis* (Oxford: Oxford University Press, 2010).

the morning star, is the lone matriarchal presence in the cosmos, invoking beauty, birth, and healing. And, finally, Saturn, who is associated in Dante with sickness and old age, is conceived as that which brings all things to an end.

Now, it is Michael Ward's thesis that the medieval cosmos of the seven heavens provides the imaginative framework for the seven books in the Narnia Chronicles. The regal splendor of Jupiter is the recurring theme throughout *The Lion, Witch, and the Wardrobe*, the chivalry of Mars -- as well as its violent abuses -- sets the stage for *Prince Caspian*, the rising of the sun in the east and the theme of gold is embodied in *The Voyage of the Dawn Treader*, the silver of the haunting moon is displayed in *The Silver Chair*, the winged foot of Mercury corresponds to Aslan's self-description as 'swift of foot' in *The Horse and His Boy*, the healing powers of Venus are embodied in the apple given to Digory to heal his mother in *The Magician's Nephew*. And in the *Last Battle*, Narnia is brought to an end by a Saturn figure of old age and death. Thus, it turns out, if Ward is correct in his thesis, and I think he absolutely is, that the Narnia Chronicles are not just wonderful fairy tales; the much beloved world of Narnia is in fact encountered through the lenses of the seven planetary moods inherent in the classical *quadriga*! And, of course, we find out that Narnia comes to an end only because it was but a shadow of a world that has no beginning nor ending. The depressing work of Saturn is replaced with the return of the regal splendor of Jupiter. Hence, we see in Narnia a world that was diaphanous of something infinitely grander and greater. London was but a microcosmic manifestation of an infinitely grand city. England was but a reflection of a land the splendor of which no mind could conceive. Thus, Lewis finishes his chronicles with these words:

The things that began to happen after that were so great and beautiful that I cannot write them. And for us this is the end of all the stories, and we can most truly say that they all lived happily ever after. But for them it was only the beginning of the real story. All their life in this world and all their adventures in Narnia had only been the cover and the title page: now at last they were beginning Chapter One of the Great Story which no one on earth has read: which goes on forever: in which every chapter is better than the one before.

It is thus the fairy tale that provides for us a picture of what education is really all about as well as a light dawning into the midst of this modernist malaise. True education would guide students into an encounter with a world that is but the cover and title page of the eternal kingdom to which they have been called; a kingdom that requires all who would enter to become as a little child, born anew. Perhaps, then, we could begin to experience the world as Chesterton did, as an arena of divine glory, celebrated in childlike wonder and awe, a veritable fountain of youth sprung from the hope of life lived happily ever after.

Part II

Practicing Wonder

CHAPTER 4

Love or Lust? How to Effectively Teach Beauty to our Students

Classical education is centered on the teaching of the True, Good, and Beautiful. As cosmic values, the student's encounter with the True, Good, and Beautiful was considered essential historically to cultivating a harmonious balance between the logical, ethical, and emotional aspects of the human soul.

And yet, this emphasis on Truth, Goodness, and Beauty is hindered by the aesthetic relativism of our modern age. I have witnessed in my own teaching experience at both the high school and university levels how modernist assumptions have worked themselves out in our aesthetic conceptions. Students as well as teachers are captive to the idea that Beauty is simply in the eye of the beholder. What you find beautiful and what I consider beautiful are merely matters of opinion. There is simply no such thing as objective Beauty.

This suggests to me that while we as parents and educators have put much thought into teaching Truth and Goodness in our classical schools, we have done so at the expense of teaching Beauty, and I am very concerned that our educational efforts are in fact being undermined by an ever-present relativism coming through the back door. Truth, Goodness, and Beauty are not sequestered from one another – they need each other and they are implied in one another. And if Beauty is robbed of its transcendent nature and relocated solely to the mere opinions of teacher and student alike, then Truth and Goodness are sure to follow.

Perhaps the most important concept our students need to learn is that, classically understood, Beauty is the delightfulness, the delectableness, the radiance of the True and Good that serves the indispensable role of drawing us toward the True and the Good. The key here is that what we find beautiful always *draws* us to something. In fact, Beauty in the classical world is a physics term; it attracts us like a gravitational pull toward something.

However, there's a problem.

The Greeks were well aware that we were not only attracted to the True and the Good; we could also be attracted to evil. They captured this in the mythologies of the Muses and the Sirens: the Muses are the daughters of Zeus who inspire Beauty and Truth, while the Sirens are water nymphs that lure sailors to their death through their bewitching songs.

And so, in order for something to be truly Beautiful, it had to be both True and Good.

So how do we tell the difference? How do we know our attractions are evoked by Beauty?

The key is found in discerning what such attraction evokes in our souls: Beauty awakens a desire to surrender oneself to the object of attraction; false beauty awakens a desire to control the object of attraction. Beauty awakens love; false beauty elicits lust. Truth attracts, lies seduce.

So, when our students are attracted to something they find beautiful, we have to teach them to discern *what* it is they are being attracted to by asking: Is it True and Good? For example, Lady Gaga music videos may attract me, but they do so in drawing me to something, namely, a world devoid of meaning and purpose that is there to be conformed to my needs and desires. This is why she is always at the center of the screen in her videos. Her artistry celebrates the emancipation of the sovereign self.

But is that True? Is that Good? Does this invite me to surrender myself in self-giving service towards the objects of my desires, or does it lure me to control them?

Of course, this is not to say that there is *nothing* True or Good about Lady Gaga's music. She is, after all, situated within 2,500 years of a musical tradition that was preserved and perfected by the church. It is to say, however, that the student needs to develop discernment when listening to her music so as to be able to approve of the Good and reject the lies.

By teaching our students how to discern the difference between two kinds of attraction, love and lust, we guide them to bring their affections in line with their commitments to the

Truth of the Christian gospel and the Goodness of their righteousness in Christ.

And that is Beautiful.

CHAPTER 5

The Secret to Fostering a Student Who Loves Your Subject

As educators, our lives can be pretty much absorbed with lesson plans and lectures, assignments and evaluations, conferences and deadlines.

Not much to love here.

Why should we expect any difference in attitude from our students?

While class and curriculum organization is of course important, it is no substitute for what classical education believed to be indispensable to fostering a love for learning subjects: *contemplation.*

Classically speaking, contemplation originally meant something akin to what goes on in a temple, such as gazing at the statue of the god. To contemplate was thus to be caught up in a divine vision. Thus, Aristotle believed that contemplation enabled the student to see the world through divine eyes.

The important point here is that contemplation was understood as that which evoked wonder and awe within the student (what the Greeks called *thauma*), and this wonder transformed into love or desire to encounter the world as a reflection of divine life. Such love was important because it served to train the affections and dispositions of the student in such a way that lives in harmony with the gods and men and thus perpetuates the life of the world.

So how do we foster contemplation within our students?

The key element to fostering contemplation within our students is teaching them to see the world as a *collection of metaphors through your own subject.*

Metaphor exemplifies the way we know the world. We all look at the world through *subsidiary* means that draw us to a *focal* point. So, I look at the world *through* my eyes, my eyes provide the subsidiary means by which I can focus on something beyond my eyes. If I start looking at my eyes, going cross-eyed as it were, I lose focus. The only way I see the world is through something that allows me to see. I think this is why we take delight in metaphor; metaphors in a sense become a new set of eyes through which we can 'see' the meaning infused in creation.

With that in mind, I want to explore 4 ways to foster the contemplative student through various subject curricula:

1. Teach them to see the world anew through stories. In the world of literature, we see through stories when we see that they point beyond themselves to a larger story, they are microcosms of a larger narrative macrocosm. Whether we are dealing with children's literature or Shakespeare, stories give us a taste of the meaning of our world through the narrative world. Thus, Shakespeare's tragedies are seen to represent the fall of humanity and his comedies represent our redemption; *Sleeping Beauty* can be seen as a story about a Christ-redeemer who slays the dragon and rescues his betrothed, by raising her to life. In *Pinocchio*, the hardened wood represents laziness, lying, and self-centeredness, and his transformation into a human represents the divine processes of regeneration and transfiguration. The *Little Mermaid* represents the quest for eternal life; *Charlotte's Web* represents life as communion and friendship.

2. Teach them to see the world anew through numbers. The Greeks, following the Pythagorean school of thought, noticed that numbers don't exist in time and space. No one has ever seen the number '1' for example; none of us have bumped into the number '1,' no one has heard, smelled it, etc. This is because the number '1' does not extend in time and space; it appears only as an adjective: one pencil, one book, one student. But the Greeks asked, what would happen to human civilization if we said that numbers and mathematics don't actually exist? We couldn't build bridges, or buildings, or roads, or anything; the regularity of the universe would be called into question; everything would collapse. So our existence, our experience of numbers is testimony to the fact that numbers and mathematics must exist, *but they must exist in another world.* And because mathematics deals with a perfect world, then it must be a divine world. So mathematics represents, literally *re*presents, that divine world in this one, and thus every time I do mathematics, I am communing with divine life, or in Augustine's refinement, the architecture of a divine mind. You see, *numbers aren't just numbers*; they point beyond themselves to something that awakens awe and wonder within us.

3. Teach them to see the world anew through shapes. In the medieval period, geometry awakened the student to divine meaning primarily through classical Christian architecture. The circular dome of the church represented heaven, with the circle representing eternity, the four corners of the floor represent the four corners of the earth, particularly Byzantine churches were a perfect square, representing the Holy of Holies, often there were four pillars that stretched down from the heavenly dome to the earthly floor which represented the four gospels testifying that heaven has come down to earth in Christ. And of course, the cruciform became the standard floor plan in the Christian west so that every church was a tangible representation of the world recreated through the cross.

4. Teach them to see the world anew through colors. Colors are highly meaningful in classical Christian art. Blue signified eternity as per the sky and the ocean depths; white signified purity and rebirth; green represents life; black represented death; red represents love as well as the fire of the Holy Spirit. For example, what color are your school uniforms? Our students are dressed in uniforms that are predominantly blue, and I never tire of reminding them what blue represents in the classical Christian consciousness; every day, when they put on their uniforms, they should be reminded that they are being prepared for eternity.

By looking not merely at but rather *through* our subjects, students will acquire a new set of eyes, ones that see the world as a divine arena of meaning and purpose redeemed in Christ, that awakens awe and wonder, and an ardent love for our subjects.

CHAPTER 6

Four Ways to Cultivate Habits of Grace in Your School

At some point in our parenting or teaching journeys, we come to the realization that education is not simply about imparting information; rather, education is formative. When we tell a child, "Don't pick your nose in public," we are doing more than merely passing on information to that child; we are shaping and cultivating the child's body and behavior, and hence fostering the child's dispositions and inclinations to act a certain way in public. Education is not merely informative, but formative of a distinct kind of human person.

This means that Christian schools must take seriously the kind of environment represented by our classrooms that is shaping the habits of students. What we want to cultivate in our students are what I call "habits of grace": dispositions, inclinations, and actions that exemplify Christ-likeness in all that they do so as to enable their humanity to flourish.

There are at least four ways to cultivate habits of grace in our students:

1. Help them see the school as sacred space. I think it is foundational that students learn to appreciate that the various practices, acts, arrangements, and etiquettes that organize and govern the life of the school collectively reveal the school as *sacred space*; a place sanctified, set apart from the world as a lived-out expression of a people in but not of the world. By understanding the school as sacred space, students will immediately realize that sacred spaces require special rules, because it is these rules that set the space apart from mundane space. *Special places require special rules.*

2. Show them that school rules let good things run wild. We have to instill within our students an appreciation that school rules and standards are not arbitrary rules that stifle their freedom; rather, rules and standards serve to cultivate their freedom. Imagine telling Michael Jordan when he was a kid, Do whatever you want with the ball, skip around with it; follow your heart and it will never let down. Instead, he was taught the *rules* of basketball. And what is the result if such rules are followed? G. K. Chesterton wrote: *"The more I considered Christianity, the more I found that while it had established a rule and order, the chief aim of that order was to give room for good things to run wild."* And so, whenever a skill is mastered, such as singing, sitting in place, obeying the teacher, compliment the students; show them how they are embodying good things that are running wild.

3. Cultivate a freedom to fast. Christ-likeness requires that we consider the needs of others as more important than our own. This in turn requires that students learn a conception of freedom that is very different from secular conceptions. Freedom in secular terms is often characterized as a negative freedom, a freedom from, or subjective freedom, the freedom to follow my heart, to do what I want to do. But in the Christian tradition, freedom is more positive, it is the ability to become what you were created to be, the freedom to fulfill our divine calling. In light of Christ's own self-giving, model before the students how considering the needs of others is more important than our own. This will both avoid conflicts as well as resolve them in a Christ-like manner.

4. Cultivate a love for honoring their teachers. We need to get our students to think through this: why are you supposed to obey your parents, your teachers, and your elders? Of course, the answer you are going to hear is because God commands it. But, remember, we want to cultivate Christ-likeness by fostering habits of grace. So *why* does God command it? Because the Son always honors the Father. The Son, as the eternal image of the Father, is always infinitely lovingly reflecting back to the Father the wisdom that the Father is always infinitely lovingly pouring into his Son. The Father did not send the Son into the world to do whatever he wanted to do. This is why you obey your elders, for in doing so you are embodying eternity and communing with divine life – you are relating to your teachers and your parents in an analogous way the Son has infinitely been relating to the Father.

Put these steps into practice, and you will be modeling before your students' habits, dispositions, and inclinations that reflect habits of grace in every area of life.

Conclusion

Thank you again for purchasing this book!

I hope this book helped you to understand and appreciate the role of wonder in education and how introducing students to such can effectively overcome cynicism and flippancy.

If you are not currently involved in a classical school or homeschooling curriculum, I would strongly urge you do so at this time. Here's a list of some organizations and associations that you can get involved with:

The Association of Classical & Christian Schools:
https://classicalchristian.org/

The Society for Classical Learning:
https://societyforclassicallearning.org/

The CiRCE Institute:
https://www.circeinstitute.org/

Scholé Academy:
http://www.classicaleducator.com/

Classical Conservations:
https://www.classicalconversations.com/

Finally, if you enjoyed this book, then I'd like to ask you for a favor, would you be kind enough to leave a review for this book on Amazon? It'd be greatly appreciated!

Thank you so much, and may God richly bless you!

Preview of *Classical vs. Modern Education: A Vision from C.S. Lewis*

I. Waterfalls and the World

There is no doubt that the 1940s constituted a most historically formidable decade: the Japanese attack on Pearl Harbor, WWII, the advent of the Atomic bomb, the transformation of the U.S. into a global super power, the establishment of NATO, the founding of the People's Republic of China. Yet among these notable events one rarely if ever comes across the inclusion of a small book, published in 1944, critiquing the state of British education. The book was entitled *The Abolition of Man*, and its author was one of the great literary minds of the twentieth-century, the renowned Oxford and Cambridge scholar, C.S. Lewis. In what is perhaps the single most significant analysis of the modern age published in the twentieth-century, Lewis in less than 100 pages outlines what Prof. Peter Kreeft calls a terrifying prophecy of mortality, not just the mortality of modern western civilization, but the mortality of human nature itself.

Lewis' critique was initiated by a textbook, which he leaves unnamed, calling it The Green Book, written by two authors he also leaves unnamed, referring to them as Gaius and Titius. The authors of this book recount the famous visit to the Waterfalls of the Clyde in Scotland taken by the poet Samuel Taylor Coleridge in the early 1800s. As Coleridge stood before the waterfall, he overheard the response of two tourists: one remarked that the waterfall was "sublime" while the other said it was "pretty." Coleridge mentally endorsed the first judgment and rejected the second with disgust. Gaius and Titius then offer their own commentary on this scene:

> When the man said *That is sublime*, he appeared to be making a remark about the waterfall.... Actually ... he was not making a remark about the waterfall, but a remark about his own feelings. What he was saying was really *I have feelings associated in my mind with the word 'Sublime'*, or shortly, *I have sublime feelings* ... This confusion is continually present in language as we use it. We appear to be saying something very important about something: and actually we are only saying something about our own feelings.

For Lewis, this comment by Gaius and Titius had nothing less than cosmic consequences. The waterfall scene and the commentary captured in microcosmic fashion *two contrasting conceptions of the world*: one, represented by Samuel Taylor Coleridge, which affirmed beauty as an objective value embedded in a created cosmic order ...

Go to http://amzn.to/2AWU7it to check out the rest of *Classical vs. Modern Education* on Amazon!

Check Out My Other Books

Below you'll find some of my other popular books that are popular on Amazon. Simply click on the links below to check them out. Alternatively, you can visit my author page on Amazon to see my other works.

- *President Trump and Our Post-Secular Future: How the 2016 Election Signals the Dawning of a Conservative Nationalist Age* http://amzn.to/2B87Q22
- *Movies and the Moral Imagination: Finding Paradise in Films* http://amzn.to/2zjghJj
- *Classical vs. Modern Education: A Vision from C.S. Lewis* http://amzn.to/2opDZju
- *Health Care Sharing Ministries: How Christians are Revolutionizing Medical Cost and Care* http://amzn.to/2B2Q8B2
- *Wise Choice: Six Steps to Godly Decision Making* http://amzn.to/2CMu1vH
- *The Face of Infinite of Love: Athanasius on the Incarnation* http://amzn.to/2oxULNM
- *Stressed Out: Learn How an Ancient Christian Practice Can Relieve Stress and Overcome Anxiety* http://amzn.to/2kFzcpc
- *Awakening Wonder: A Classical Guide to Truth, Goodness, and Beauty* http://amzn.to/2ziKR5H
- *Worldview Guide for* A Christmas Carol http://amzn.to/2BCcKHO
- *The Ritualized Revelation of the Messianic Age: Washings and Meals in Galatians and 1 Corinthians* http://amzn.to/2B0mGvf

If the links do not work, for whatever reason, you can simply search for these titles on the Amazon website to find them.

About www.TurleyTalks.com

Are we seeing the revitalization of Christian civilization?
For decades, the world has been dominated by a process known as globalization, an economic and political system that hollows out and erodes a culture's traditions, customs, and religions, all the while conditioning populations to rely on the expertise of a tiny class of technocrats for every aspect of their social and economic lives.

Until now.

All over the world, there's been a massive blowback against the anti-cultural processes of globalization and its secular aristocracy. From Russia to Europe and now in the U.S., citizens are rising up and reasserting their religion, culture, and nation as mechanisms of resistance against the dehumanizing tendencies of secularism and globalism.

And it's just the beginning.

The secular world is at its brink, and a new traditionalist age is rising.
Join me each week as we examine these worldwide trends, discover answers to today's toughest challenges, and together learn to live in the present in light of even better things to come.

So hop on over to www.TurleyTalks.com and have a look around. Make sure to sign-up for our weekly Email Newsletter where you'll get lots of free giveaways, private Q&As, and tons of great content. Check out our YouTube channel (www.youtube.com/c/DrSteveTurley) where you'll understand current events in light of conservative trends to help you flourish in your personal and professional life. And of course, 'Like' us on Facebook and follow us on Twitter.

Thank you so much for your support and for your part in this cultural renewal.

About the Author

Steve Turley (PhD, Durham University) is an internationally recognized scholar, speaker, and classical guitarist. He is the author of *Awakening Wonder: A Classical Guide to Truth, Goodness, and Beauty* (Classical Academic Press) and *The Ritualized Revelation of the Messianic Age: Washings and Meals in Galatians and 1 Corinthians* (T&T Clark). Steve blogs on the church, society and culture, education, and the arts at TurleyTalks.com. He is a faculty member at Tall Oaks Classical School in Bear, DE, where he teaches Theology, Greek, and Rhetoric, and Professor of Fine Arts at Eastern University. Steve lectures at universities, conferences, and churches throughout the U.S. and abroad. His research and writings have appeared in such journals as *Christianity and Literature, Calvin Theological Journal, First Things, Touchstone,* and *The Chesterton Review.* He and his wife, Akiko, have four children and live in Newark, DE, where they together enjoy fishing, gardening, and watching *Duck Dynasty* marathons.

Made in the USA
Middletown, DE
13 November 2021